Sushi

MARLISA SZWILLUS
KUNISUKE MITANI

Photographer
BARBARA BORISOLLI

Published by Mud Puddle Books, Inc., 54 West 21st Street, Suite 601 New York, NY 10010
Published originally under the title SUSHI-Der pure Genuss © 2000 by Gräfe und Unzer Verlag GmbH, München.
English translation copyright © 2003 by Mud Puddle Books, Inc. All rights reserved.
Reprints, even in parts, as well as distributing by means of film, radio and TV, photomechanical reproduction,
sound carrier and data processing systems in any form are allowed only with prior written permission from the publisher.

Editing: Sabine Sälzer • Cover Designer: Claudia Fillmann • Photographs: Barbara Bonisolli

Marlisa Szwillus works as a self-employed specialized journalist and book author in Munich, is a member of the Food-Editors-Club. As an Asia-loving author, who has detailed knowledge about Far Eastern cuisine, she already gave beginners an appetizing introduction to Sushi with her book *Sushi leicht gemacht*. **Barbara Bonisolli** belongs to the new generation of food photographers. In addition to good food she is interested in everything beautiful that relates to table and kitchen. That is why Barbara Bonisolli designs the appealing ambiance for her photographs herself. **Kunisuke Mitani**, Sushi master in the renowned Munich Japanese restaurant Tokami, was responsible for the food styling at the photoproduction.

ISBN: 1-59412-029-3 • Made in China.

MUD PUDDLE BOOKS, INC.
New York, New York

Contents

Pure Joy

The popularity of finger food in restaurants and at home is spreading throughout the world. Now you can spoil yourself and your guests with sushi, a thrilling culinary joy that is easier to make than you imagine.

The Classics of Japanese Cuisine

In our part of the world sushi is the most visible representation of the Japanese kitchen. Sushi evokes images of food that is natural, harmonious and esthetically pleasing. In preparing sushi we try not to alter the ingredients more than necessary in order to preserve the original taste. Seasonal ingredients are preferred. The harmony of sushi comes from the interplay between the taste, consistency and colors of the ingredients. The esthetics of sushi are demonstrated by the high standards of arrangement and decoration. What appears artistic and unusual to us is commonplace in Japan. In spite of a high-tech society and the proliferation of fast food, people in Japan remain faithful to the their traditional food culture and view it as an integral piece of art in their lives.

More Than a Trend

Recently we have been witness to a worldwide sushi boom. Sushi bars have multiplied in cities of all sizes and restaurant hot spots find that they must feature a sushi menu. Food lovers everywhere are discovering the joys of sushi and celebrating these new culinary delights. Sushi rolls are deliciously filled and decorated with an incredible amount of possibilities including tender and delicate fish, raw and cooked ingredients, vegetables and omelettes. Sushi is no longer the hidden secret of a small circle of food insiders. It has become an up-scale food for everyone. More and more enthusiastic sushi fans are making and enjoying their gourmet treats at home. This book presents detailed recipes so that even an inexperienced sushi cook can try them with great success. In addition to being delicious, sushi looks visually perfect. This is a combination that will delight your guests who will echo in astonishment, "You really made this yourself?"

Healthy and Body Friendly

Nutritionists praise sushi as a balanced and incredibly healthy food. Fish and seafood deliver a full spectrum of nutrients and are extremely low in fat. The nutrients supplied support mental and physical strength. They provide easy to digest proteins, vitamins, minerals and omega-3 fatty acids that, according to some studies, help prevent heart disease and circulatory problems. Rice and vegetables deliver important fibers and carbohydrates. Nori, which is made of pressed seaweed, contains an unusual amount of minerals and vitamins especially iodine and vitamin B-12. This is important for vegetarians because normally only animal foods contain vitamin B-12. In general, sushi promotes health and a healthy looking body.

How to Eat Sushi

A small bowl with soy sauce is handed to everyone. Wasabi paste, a spicy green horseradish, is added to the soy sauce. Additionally, pickled ginger is served to use between bites. The ginger has a neutralizing and refreshing effect. The same effect can be achieved with a sip of Miso Soup (see recipe page 78), green tea or water.

Sushi is dipped in soy sauce and eaten in one bite. Only Temaki is eaten in small bites. It's common in Japan to eat Nigiri-, Hosomaki-, Uramaki-Sushi and Gunkan-Maki with both chopsticks and fingers. However, using a fork and knife is frowned upon. Always use your fingers for Temaki. Sashimi, Chirashi and steamed sushi are generally eaten with chopsticks.

Which Drinks Accompany Sushi?

The delicate taste of green tea blends well with sushi. Saki, a rice wine served in small bottles, is also a good accompaniment. The saki is warmed in hot water and served in a tiny porcelain cup. On hot days saki is sometimes served ice cold. It's also common to serve beer with sushi (domestic or Japanese beer are fine). Mineral water is also suitable.

The Perfect Sushi Kitchen

Important Ingredients

You will find the following Japanese ingredients in a good supermarket as well as in Asian food markets.

Pictured from left to right:

Nori seaweed: Made from dried and pressed seaweed. These green, wafer-thin leaves are wrapped around Maki- and Temaki-Sushi. If possible, buy nori seaweed toasted and ready to use.

Sushi-rice: This special type of rice gets sticky after cooking and is therefore easy to form. If sushi-rice is not available, it's possible to use round grain rice. Other types of rice will not work with sushi.

Sesame seeds: White sesame seeds are usually toasted and used as a spice while dark sesame seeds are used only for decoration.

Shiitake mushrooms: Also known under the Chinese name Tongu mushroom. Dried shiitakes are spicier than fresh ones. Try to find mushrooms with "fat" caps. The mushrooms are prepared in a spicy broth. Shiitake mushrooms are used as fillings or toppings.

Kombu: A type of seaweed that is sold dried in somewhat thicker sheets than nori seaweed Kombu is used for the preparation of the sushi-rice.

Kampyo: Dried pumpkin in long thin strips. The pumpkin is soaked in water and then simmered in a spicy broth. Used as a filling or topping.

Pictured left to right:

Sake: Japanese rice wine. Not only a traditional drink but also an important ingredient.

Rice vinegar (Su): Used as a seasoning for sushi-rice. Japanese rice vinegar is far milder than domestic vinegars. If necessary you can use a highly diluted domestic vinegar.

Mirin: Sweet rice wine used only for seasoning You can substitute Spanish sherry if necessary.

Soy sauce: The basic Japanese seasoning sauce. Soy sauce can be either salty or slightly sweet. Use the dark, salty variety for sushi.

Dashi: Instant fish stock.

In the front picture:

Wasabi: Extra spicy green horseradish. You can buy it as a ready-made paste or as a powder that is mixed with water.

Pickled ginger (Shoga): Pickled in vinegar, ginger can be kept in the refrigerator for weeks.

Typical Tools

These are the most important utensils needed for the preparation of sushi. Certain tools are not always necessary but make the work a lot easier. Alternatives may be found in every household. Typical sushi tools may be found in any Japanese or Asian store or food market.

Pictured from bottom to top:

Cutting board: Use a big, stable cutting board. Bamboo rice paddle: Necessary for mixing the rice and vinegar.

Kitchen Knife: An extremely sharp, long, thin blade is used to cut fish in clean and precise slices. A broader knife is used for vegetables and other ingredients.

Chopsticks: Used to stir ingredients (you may also use a spoon or fork).

Tweezers: To remove fish bones.

Wooden bowl (Hangiri): This is useful in removing excess liquid from the rice. An unfinished wooden salad bowl or a stoneware bowl may also be used.

Fan: Use a fan to quickly cool the rice.

Bamboo rolling-mat (Makisu): This mat is the ideal tool for forming sushi rolls.

Bamboo steamer: These stackable steamers are highly suitable for steaming Mushi-Sushi.

MAKI-SUSHI

Roll-Play Japanese Style

Maki-Sushi stirs the joy of discovery. They are a refined and exciting delicacy with a plain beauty that is a visual delight. With so many varied fillings Maki-Sushi keep us asking for more.

Kitchen Roles and Filling Rolls

An old Japanese proverb predicts that we will live 75 days longer if we are lucky enough to taste something we have never eaten before. This luck will be found in abundance in the endless variations of Maki-Sushi. Maki-Sushi typically uses nori seaweed, which is sheets of dried and pressed seaweed. With the help of a rolling mat you can roll sticky rice onto the nori sheet. This is the way the spicy fillings will be covered. The sushi filling determines the taste and can include fish, caviar, seafood, omelette, vegetables, mushrooms, lettuce and herbs. Sushi rolls are cut into handy pieces when finished. Form and size of the rolls vary.

From Hoso- to Furo-Maki

Sushi made from half a nori sheet is called Hoso-Maki (thin sushi rolls) while sushi made from a whole sheet is called Foto-Maki (thick sushi rolls). Ura-Maki refers to the interesting "inside-out rolls" where the order of ingredients is reversed. In other words, the nori seaweed is on the inside and the rice on the outside.

Gunkan-Maki, which means "sushi in the form of a battleship", always has a filling with a soft consistency. In order to keep the filling from slipping out or dissolving, a rice ball is tied together with an oversized strip of nori seaweed. This creates a stable "wall" to hold the filling.

Following Your Own Taste

A sushi-meal follows no strict rules except your own desires. You might find, however, that if you have prepared different types of sushi (for example, a selection of Maki- and Nigiri-Sushi) you might want to eat the Maki-Sushi first since the crisp nori sheet will be softened by the wet rice and filling over time.

Helpful Hints

• Strong aluminum foil moistened with vinegar water can serve as a substitute for a rolling mat.

• Wet the inside of your hands and fingers with a vinegar water mix when preparing Maki-Sushi. Otherwise the sticky rice will really live up to its name.

• The rice must be at room temperature. If the rice is too warm the nori sheets will curl and cold rice will not stick together.

• Instead of using your hand, you can spread sushi-rice on the nori sheet with a spoon. Keep dipping the spoon into a vinegar-water mix while spreading the rice onto the sheet. Use soft strokes so that the rice will not get mashed.

• Beginners may find it easier to spread the wasabi paste on the nori sheet instead of spreading it on the rice. If children are participating either in the preparation or the eating, you may leave out the wasabi paste.

• If you make sushi often you may find it worthwhile to prepare larger amounts of seasoned pumpkin and marinated shiitake mushrooms. They will keep in a sealed jar in the refrigerator for several weeks.

• You can use leftovers from the preparation of Nigiri-Sushi for Maki-Sushi; for example, slices of fish filet and strips of omelette.

• Sushi rolls may be cut in various ways to provide visual variety.

Multicultural Mix for More Culinary Delights

For the most part the following recipes have classical Japanese fillings. However, the successful mixture of domestic cuisine adds joy and pleasure to a meal. For example, the California roll (see recipe page 22) with avocado and crab is an American sushi variation. So feel free to be creative and put together new fillings dictated by your own taste.

Quantity

For appetizers and snacks you can plan on using one sushi roll per person. The sushi roll may be cut into four or six pieces depending on the thickness and the filling. Two Gunkan-Maki make a portion. If you don't intend to serve other kinds of sushi, like Nigiri- or Temaki-Sushi, you may want to increase the portions three or four times to satisfy everyone's appetite.

Hosomaki-Sushi with Carrots and Cucumbers

Low budget • To the left in the picture

Ingredients for 24 pieces
1 big carrot • 1 piece of cucumber or zucchini (about 4 inches/10 cm) • 3 tbsp sake (Japanese rice wine) • $1/_2$ tsp sugar • $1/_4$ tsp salt • 2 toasted nori sheets • $2\,2/_3$ cups (400 g) prepared sushi-rice (see recipe page 74) • 1 tsp wasabi paste
Serve with: soy sauce • wasabi paste • pickled ginger

Cooking time: 30 minutes
Calories: one piece 25 calories

Peel the carrot and cut lengthwise in about $1/_4$ inch ($1/_2$ cm) slices, then cut them in $1/_4$ inch ($1/_2$ cm) strips. Wash the cucumber/zucchini and dry it. Cut off the peel about a $1/_4$ inch thick. Then cut it into $1/_4$ inch ($1/_2$ cm) wide strips.

Let sake, 2 tbsp water, sugar and salt come to a boil in a pan. Add the carrot strips and let simmer with a lid for 1 minute. Remove it from the heat and add cucumber/zucchini strips to the carrots. Let it cool in the broth. Take out the vegetables and pat dry with paper towel.

Cut each nori sheet in half. With the rolling mat prepare the Maki-Sushi with the ingredients, the rice and the wasabi paste. Cut the sushi rolls into six pieces each. Arrange and decorate.

Hosomaki-Sushi with Pumpkin

Vegetarian • To the right in the picture

Ingredients for 16 pieces
$1/_3$ oz (10 g) dried pumpkin or dried gourd • 1 tsp salt • $2/_3$ cups (150 ml) dashi (instant fish stock) or water • 2 tsp sugar • 2 tbsp soy sauce • 1 tbsp mirin (Japanese cooking wine) • 2 toasted nori sheets • $2\,2/_3$ cups (400 g) prepared sushi-rice (see recipe page 74)
Serve with: soy sauce • wasabi paste • pickled ginger

Cooking time: 1 hour (allow an extra 20 minutes for soaking)
Calories: one piece 30 calories

Rinse the pumpkin. Rub it between your hands with salt until it softens. Rinse off. Let the pumpkin soak in water for at least 20 minutes. Pour out the water and then cover the pumpkin with fresh water, let it come to a boil and simmer for 10 minutes, drain.

Put the pumpkin together with the dashi or water in a pan. Add sugar, soy sauce and mirin. Let it simmer uncovered over low heat, until almost all liquid has evaporated. Let the pumpkin cool off and pat dry with a paper towel.

Cut the nori sheets crosswise in half. Using the rolling mat form the Maki-Sushi with the prepared pumpkin and the rice. Cut the sushi rolls in 4 equally large pieces.

Hosomaki-Sushi with Shiitake Mushrooms

Exquisite • In front of picture

Ingredients for 16 pieces
4 medium dried shiitake mushrooms (4-6 g) • 1 tbsp
sugar • 3 tbsp soy sauce • 2 tbsp mirin (Japanese
cooking wine) • 1 scallion • 2 toasted nori sheets •
$2^2/_3$ cups (400 g) prepared sushi-rice (see recipe
page 74) • 1 tsp wasabi paste
Serve with: soy sauce • wasabi paste • pickled ginger

**Cooking time: 1 hour (allow an extra 20 minutes
for soaking)**
Calories: one piece 35 calories

Cover the mushrooms with $^2/_3$ cups (150 ml) boiling
water and let soak for 20 min. Then pour into a small
strainer. Retain the water for later. Rinse the mushrooms
carefully and remove the hard stems.

Bring the mushroom-soaking water, sugar, soy sauce
and mirin to a boil. Let the mushrooms simmer in this
broth for 10 minutes. Stir occasionally. Drain and let
them drip dry. Cut the mushroom caps into strips.

Wash, clean and dry the scallion, then cut into tiny
rings. Cut each nori sheet crosswise in half. Prepare
Maki-Sushi, using the rolling mat, by mixing the prepared ingredients, the rice and the wasabi paste. Cut
the sushi rolls into four equally large pieces and arrange
them with the cut edge facing up.

Hosomaki-Sushi with Cucumber and Sesame

Easy to prepare • In the back of the picture

Ingredients for 24 pieces
4 tsp sesame seeds • 1 piece of cucumber (about
4 inches/10 cm long) • 2 toasted nori sheets • $2^2/_3$
cups (400 g) prepared sushi-rice (see recipe page 74) •
1 tsp wasabi paste
Serve with: soy sauce • wasabi paste • pickled ginger

Cooking time: 25 minutes
Calories: one piece 20 calories

Toast the sesame seeds in a small pan without oil on
medium heat. Stir until golden brown. Remove from
pan, put it aside and let cool.

Wash and dry the cucumber. Cut with the peel in
$^1/_4$ inch ($^1/_2$ cm) pieces with a long knife. Then cut
these in $^1/_4$ inch ($^1/_2$ cm) strips. Cut the nori sheets
crosswise in two halves. Prepare the Maki-Sushi with
a rolling mat and mix all the prepared ingredients with
the prepared rice and the wasabi paste. Cut the 4 sushi
rolls into 6 equally large pieces and arrange them with
the cut edges facing up.

Hosomaki-Sushi with Salmon and Avocado

Easy to make • To the left in the picture

Ingredients for 24 pieces
1 bundle of chives • $^1/_4$ ripe avocado • 1 tsp lemon juice • about 5 oz (125 g) fresh salmon filet without skin (preferably organic) • 2 toasted nori sheets • $2^2/_3$ cups (400 g) prepared sushi-rice (see recipe page 74) • 1 tsp wasabi paste
Serve with: soy sauce • wasabi paste • pickled ginger

Cooking time: 25 minutes
Calories: one piece 65 calories

Wash the chives and dry with a cloth. Don't cut them. Peel the $^1/_4$ of the avocado and cut it lengthwise into 8 strips. Drip some lemon juice immediately on the avocado strips so they don't turn brown. Dry off the salmon filet and cut it lengthwise in $^1/_4$ inch ($^1/_2$ cm) wide strips. Cut the nori sheets across in half.

Use a rolling mat to prepare the Maki-Sushi with the rice, the wasabi paste and the ingredients.

Hosomaki-Sushi with Crisp Salmon

Exquisite • To the right in the picture

Ingredients for 16 pieces
8 small lettuce leaves • 1 piece of cucumber (about 4 inches/10 cm) • about $^2/_3$ lb (300 g) of fresh salmon filet with skin (preferably organic) • 1 tbsp corn starch powder • 3 tbsp oil • 2 toasted nori sheets • $2^2/_3$ cups (400 g) prepared sushi-rice (see recipe page 74) • 1 tsp wasabi paste
Serve with: soy sauce • wasabi paste • pickled ginger

Cooking time: 35 minutes
Calories: one piece 81 calories

Wash the lettuce and dry with a paper towel. Wash and dry the cucumber. Cut it with the peel in $^1/_4$ inch ($^1/_2$ cm) pieces, then cut them in $^1/_4$ inch ($^1/_2$ cm) thick strips.

Dry the salmon, powder it with starch. Fry it with the skin two minutes until crisp in heated oil on medium heat, turn it and fry it for another minute. Take it out of the pan and dry off the fat. Cut the salmon lengthwise in strips. Cut the nori sheets diagonally in half.

Use the rolling mat to make Maki-Sushi with the prepared ingredients, the rice and the wasabi paste. Put the ingredients on the thin side of the nori sheet. Let the lettuce and the cucumber stick out at the ends. Cut the rolls in 4 pieces each.

Hosomaki-Sushi with Chopped Tuna

Easy to make • In the front of picture

Ingredients for 24 pieces
1 spring onion or 2 oz (40 g) new leeks • about 5 oz (125 g) fresh tuna filet • 2 toasted nori sheets • 2 $^2/_3$ cups (400 g) prepared sushi-rice (see recipe page 74) • 1 tsp wasabi paste.
Serve with: soy sauce • wasabi paste • pickled ginger

Cooking time: 30 minutes
Calories: one piece 30 calories

Wash, clean and dry the onion/leek, then cut into small pieces. Dry off the tuna filet and cut into cubes. Using a sharp knife, combine the onion/leek and the tuna cubes and chop them on a plastic board. Cut the nori sheets across in half.

Use a rolling mat to make the Maki-Sushi with the prepared ingredients, the rice and the wasabi paste. Cut the sushi rolls each in 6 equally large pieces. Arrange them with the cut surface facing up.

Hosomaki-Sushi with Marinated Tuna

Spicy • In the rear of picture

Ingredients for 24 pieces
About 5 oz (125 g) fresh tuna filet • 2 tsp low fat mayonnaise • 1 tsp sesame oil • 1 tsp rice vinegar • $^1/_4$ tsp shichimi togarashi (hot seasoning) • 2 toasted nori sheets • 2 $^2/_3$ cups (400 g) prepared sushi-rice (see recipe page 74)
For decoration: shichimi togarashi • chopped onion or chives
Serve with: soy sauce • wasabi paste • pickled ginger

Cooking time: 30 minutes
Calories: one piece 30 calories

Dry off the fish filet and cut into $^1/_2$ inch (1 cm) thick strips. Mix the mayonnaise, sesame oil, rice vinegar and seasoning in a flat bowl. Turn the tuna strips in the bowl, cover and leave them to marinate for 5 minutes. Meanwhile, cut the nori sheets across in half.

Use a rolling mat to make Maki-Sushi with the marinated tuna fish and the prepared rice. Cut the sushi rolls in 6 equally large pieces. Arrange them with the cut surface facing up. Decorate, if you wish, with seasoning, chopped onion or chives.

Futo-Maki with Prawns, Omelette and Mushrooms

More time consuming

Ingredients for 8-12 Pieces

4 medium dried shiitake mushrooms (4-6 g) • 1 tbsp sugar • 3 tbsp soy sauce • 4 tbsp mirin (Japanese cooking wine) • salt • 4 oz (100 g) spinach leaves • 4 medium boiled and peeled prawns (20 g each) • 1 piece of cucumber (about 2 inches/5 cm) • 4 pumpkin or dried gourd strips (prepared, see instructions and helpful hints page 12) • 3 toasted nori sheets • $1^2/_3$ cups (240 g) prepared sushi-rice (see recipe page 74) Serve with: soy sauce, wasabi paste, pickled ginger

Cooking time: 50 minutes (allow an extra 20 minutes for soaking)
Calories: one piece 50 calories (if cut in 12 pieces)

Soak the dried mushrooms in $^2/_3$ cups (150 ml) hot water for 20 min. Drain and retain the water. Rinse the mushrooms thoroughly and remove the hard stems.

Combine mushroom-soaking water, sugar, soy sauce and 2 tbsp mirin and bring to a boil. Let the mushrooms simmer in the broth for 10 min. Pour in a strainer and let it drain.

Bring salted water to a boil in a pan while the mushrooms are simmering. Wash the spinach and let boil for 30 seconds. Drain in ice cold water, then dry and toss the spinach leaves. Cut the prawns lengthwise in half, toss them in the leftover mirin.

Wash and dry the cucumber piece. Using a long knife cut it with the peel into a $^1/_2$ inch (1 cm) thick piece. Then cut it into $^1/_2$ inch (1 cm) thick strips. Cut the marinated shiitake mushrooms into strips. Dry off the prepared pumpkin strips. Cut the prepared omelette into about $^1/_2$ inch (1 cm) thick strips.

Use a rolling mat to make large Maki-Sushi (see recipe page 76). Place a whole nori sheet on the rolling mat. Dip your hands in water. Spread half of the prepared sushi-rice on the sheet. Leave a margin on each side. Cut a second nori sheet crosswise in half. Cover the rice with one half of the nori sheet so that it touches the bottom side of the other half. Press the sheet on to the other half. Place half of the prepared ingredients crosswise on the nori. Form everything into a thick roll. Make a second roll from the rest of the ingredients. Cut the two sushi rolls into 4-6 pieces each.

Helpful Hint

It is good to combine this recipe with "Nigiri-Sushi with Omelette" (see recipe page 42). This way you can use 3 oz (80 g) from this omelette. The omelette can also be substituted with $^1/_2$ inch (1 cm) thick blanched carrot sticks.

Ura-Maki-Sushi: California Roll

Exquisite • For more experienced cooks

Ingredients for 24 Pieces
3 tbsp sesame seeds • 4 crab sticks (about 60g) • one piece of cucumber (about 4 inches/10 cm) • $^1/_4$ of a ripe avocado • 1 tsp lemon juice • 2 toasted nori sheets • $1^2/_3$ cups (240 g) prepared sushi-rice (see recipe page 74) • 1 tbsp low fat mayonnaise
Serve with: soy sauce • wasabi paste • pickled ginger

Cooking time: 30 minutes
Calories: one piece 20 calories

Toast the sesame seeds without oil in a small pan on low heat until golden brown. Stir occasionally. Remove from the pan and let cool.

Dry off the crab sticks and cut them lengthwise in half. Wash and dry the cucumber. Cut it with the peel in one $^1/_4$ inch ($^1/_2$ cm) thick piece, using a long knife. Then cut into $^1/_4$ inch ($^1/_2$ cm) thick strips.

Peel the avocado piece, cut into strips. Immediately sprinkle some lemon juice on them so that they don't turn brown.

Cover the rolling mat with plastic foil. Place a nori sheet on it with the smooth side facing down. Dip your hands in water and spread half of the sushi-rice on the nori sheet. Leave a margin on the upper and lower side of the sheet. Turn the sheet over carefully so that the rice is now facing down and the nori sheet up (see instructions page 77).

Spread a thin layer of mayonnaise along the lower third of the sheet. Cover with half of the crab sticks, the cucumber and avocado strips. Roll up the rice, the nori sheet and the filling with the mat. Prepare a second roll in the same manner, with the rest of the ingredients. Cut the sushi rolls into 6 equally large pieces. Dip one side of each piece in the toasted sesame seeds.

Variation
Ura-Maki with Salmon
Clean a large carrot for the filling. Cut into finger thick sticks and blanch in boiling water. Blanch 4 oz (100 g) of whole spinach leaves in salt water. Drain and run in cold water, squeeze or toss until dry. Cut 4 oz (100 g) salmon filet in finger-thick strips and marinate in some mirin. Prepare according to the recipe.

Gunkan-Maki with Shrimps

To the left in the picture

Ingredients for 8 pieces
About 5 oz (150 g) shrimp • 1 tbsp low fat mayonnaise •
2 tsp mirin (Japanese cooking wine) • 2 tsp lemon juice
• 2 bundles of chives • 2 toasted nori sheets • $1^2/_3$
cups (240 g) prepared sushi-rice (see recipe page 74) •
1 tsp wasabi paste
Serve with: soy sauce • wasabi paste • pickled ginger

Cooking time: 20 minutes
Calories: one piece 65 calories

Pat the shrimp dry with a paper towel and cut them into
medium-sized pieces. Mix them with mayonnaise, mirin,
and lemon juice. Wash and drain the chives. Cut the
chives into $2^1/_2$ inch (6-7 cm) strips. Trim any frazzled
edges from the nori sheets and cut them lengthwise in
eight $1^1/_4$ inch (3 cm) thick and 6 inch (15 cm) long
strips.

Dip your hands in water. Form the sushi-rice into 8 oval
rice balls. Wrap a strip of the nori sheet around each rice
ball with the smooth side of the sheet facing outwards.
Stick the ends of the sheet together with some rice.

Press the rice gently onto the nori sheet. Spread $3/_4$ of the
shrimp evenly over the rice. Top with 6-7 chives. Place the
rest of the shrimp on top. Take a small amount of wasabi
paste, form 8 little beads and decorate the sushi.

Gunkan-Maki with Salmon-Caviar

A classic • To the right in the picture

Ingredients for 8 Pieces
2 toasted nori sheets • $1^2/_3$ cups (240 g) prepared
sushi-rice (see recipe page 74) • about 3 oz (80 g)
salmon caviar • 4 diagonally thin-cut pieces of
cucumber • 1 tsp wasabi paste
Serve with: soy sauce • wasabi paste • pickled ginger

Cooking time: 20 minutes
Calories: one piece 45 calories

Trim the ends of the nori seaweed. Cut the sheets into
8 strips about $1^1/_4$ inch (3 cm) thick and 6 inch (15 cm)
long.

Dip your hands in vinegar water. Form the sushi-rice into
8 oval rice balls. Wrap a strip of the nori sheet around
each rice ball with the smooth side facing outwards.
Stick the sheet together with one or two grains of rice.

Press down the rice on the nori sheet carefully and
spread the caviar evenly.

Cut the cucumber slices in half, then cut out fan like
slices and stick them between the rice and the caviar.
Form 8 little beads with the wasabi paste and decorate
the sushi.

NIGIRI-SUSHI

Culinary Artistry

It's fascinating to watch a Japanese sushi chef forming Nigiri-Sushi with elegant yet quick movements. It may look daunting but, with some persistence and practice, anyone can conquer the basics.

The Original Form of Sushi

Sushi has been mentioned in Japanese literature for centuries. Originally, sushi stood for fish and clams pickled for preservation. Over time rice was added to provide more taste for the fish. In the 19th century the prototype of Nigiri-Sushi as we know it today appeared. Traveling vendors put a slice of raw fish on a vinegared rice ball and sold their creations on the roadside as an inexpensive snack. Sushi was often packed and brought home in boxes. Times have changed. Sushi is now generally reserved as a treat for special occasions.

Variety

When we refer to sushi we generally mean Nigiri-Sushi. This is true even in Japan. However, each region in Japan has its own specialties contributing to the great variety of sushi. Only a small portion of this vast selection is offered in our sushi bars. In our part of the world, hand-made Nigiri-Sushi is the most beloved and popular sushi.

The Joy Begins at the Fish Market

Generally, you need only a few ingredients for sushi preparation, but the ingredients need to be the best quality and absolutely fresh. This is particularly true if you use raw fish for a filling or topping. Tell the fish merchant that you intend to eat the fish raw and require "sushi quality filet". Fresh fish has firm meat that will give a bit if you squeeze it with your finger. The cut should be smooth and shimmering. Remember that absolutely fresh fish does not have a fishy smell. It should have a pleasant and appetizing smell of ocean. If you need to, you can keep the fish filet in plastic foil for one day in the refrigerator. If you use frozen fish or seaweed, you should unwrap it, place it on a plate, cover it and let it thaw in the refrigerator. When thawed, rinse it well and dry thoroughly with a paper towel.

Helpful Hints for the Preparation

Even though Nigiri-Sushi is, in theory, the easiest sushi to prepare, a Japanese sushi-chef needs years of training before completely mastering the art of serving this gourmet treat. However, with practice, everyone is able to present attractive samples of sushi. You'll find a guide to forming sushi step-by-step in the back section of this book. Remember to make certain that a raw fish topping doesn't get warm while forming the sushi. Ideally you should eat sushi minutes after preparing it. This is easy to achieve in a sushi bar but harder at home. Nigiri-Sushi can be prepared up to two hours before dinner. Cover the finished sushi pieces with plastic wrap and keep them in the refrigerator. They should be served at room temperature.

How to Serve and Arrange Sushi

Strict rules and skills dictate how sushi is served in Japan. However, at home we can take a more relaxed approach. You should know, though, that Nigiri-Sushi is served in pairs (two pieces per person). The selection should include as many "colors" as possible; for instance, "red" for red tuna, "white" for all fish with white meat, "blue" for the blue-shimmering skin of mackerel and sardines, "orange" for salmon and "yellow" for river eel and omelette.

How to Eat Nigiri-Sushi

If you're comfortable with chopsticks, tip the Nigiri-Sushi on its side and pick it up so that it can be easily dipped in the soy sauce (seasoned with wasabi to taste). Don't dip the part with the rice in the sauce (this will cause the rice to crumble). Also, don't sprinkle soy sauce over the sushi roll. If you prefer eating sushi with your fingers, put the pointer finger on the back end of the filling. Then pick up the sushi using your thumb and middle finger. Dip in the soy sauce.

Nigiri-Sushi with Tuna

Easy to make • A classic

Ingredients for 8 Pieces
About 5 oz (150 g) fresh tuna (choose from "otoro",
"chutoro" or "akami" (see Hints) • 2 tsp wasabi paste •
1 cup (150 g) prepared sushi-rice (see recipe page 74)
Serve with: soy sauce • wasabi paste • pickled ginger

Cooking time: 25 minutes
Calories: one piece 60 calories

Pat the tuna dry with a paper towel. Remove any
remaining fish bones with tweezers. Trim frazzled
ends. Cut the fish slightly diagonally against the
grain, as exactly as possible in 8 thin $1^1/_4$ x 2 inch
(3 x 5 cm) slices.

Spread some wasabi paste with the tip of your finger
on one side of the fish slices. Dip your hands in water
and form 8 finger-shaped rice balls with the sushi-rice.
Assemble the Nigiri-Sushi with the prepared ingredients
as described in the instructions. Serve as soon as
possible.

Hints

Tuna fish is a classic sushi filling and is also the most
popular. Sushi beginners are often surprised that the
tuna doesn't really taste like "fish". Its taste reminds
many people of beef or veal. Apart from the various tuna
types, it also depends on which part of the fish is used.
The tuna parts differ not only in taste, but also in color
and price. In Japan, and in many of the worldwide sushi
bars, you can choose between three different tuna parts.
"Otoro" is greatly appreciated and is light colored and
rich in fat. Since it is the first choice for insiders, it is
accordingly expensive. "Chutoro" is also a cut from the
belly, the meat has less fat and has a medium red color.
"Akami" on the other hand is deep red and lean. This
piece is cut from the back of the fish. Try all three and
decide which cut you like the most.

Nigiri-Sushi with Salmon

In the front of picture

Ingredients for 8 Pieces
About 5 oz (150 g) fresh salmon filet • 2 tsp wasabi paste • 1 cup (150 g) prepared sushi-rice (see recipe page 74) • 2 tbsp salmon caviar
Serve with: soy sauce • wasabi paste • pickled ginger

Cooking time: 25 minutes
Calories: one piece 60 calories

Cut the salmon filet at a slight diagonal against the grain into 8 thin, even pieces about $1^1/_4$ x 2 inches (3 x 5 cm). This is easier if the filet is slightly frozen. This can be achieved by leaving the fish in aluminum foil in the freezer for about 1 hour.

Spread a thin layer of wasabi paste on one side when the salmon is defrosted, but still cold. Dip your hands in water and form 8 longish rice balls with the sushi-rice. Complete the Nigiri-Sushi as described in the instructions. Decorate with salmon caviar, arrange and serve as soon as possible.

Hint
Connoisseurs choose Irish wild or organic salmon. The organic salmon is bred according to its type and under strict ecological guidelines. The fish is not given any supplements, hormones or medication. Therefore, the meat is firm and incomparably aromatic.

Nigiri-Sushi with Prawns

Somewhat expensive • In the rear of picture

Ingredients for 8 pieces
8 medium raw and unpeeled prawns (about 30g each, fresh or frozen) • salt • 2 tbsp rice vinegar • 2 tbsp mirin (Japanese cooking wine) • 2 tsp wasabi paste • 1 cup (150 g) prepared sushi-rice (see recipe page 74)
In addition: 8 wooden barbecue sticks
Serve with: soy sauce • wasabi paste • pickled ginger

Cooking time; 30 minutes
Calories: one piece 50 calories

Stick the fresh or defrosted prawns on the barbecue sticks, bottom first. Place them in boiling salted water on low heat for 3-4 min. Remove them from the saucepan and rinse in ice cold water.

Remove the sticks. Peel the prawns. Make a slit length-wise in the back and remove the dark back vein. Now cut the belly lengthwise, without cutting through and pull it open like a butterfly. Combine rice vinegar and mirin. Marinate the prawns in the vinegar mix for 3 minutes. Remove and dry with paper towel.

Spread a very thin layer of wasabi paste on the lower half. Dip your hands in water and form the sushi-rice into 8 finger shaped rice balls. Make the Nigiri-Sushi with the prepared ingredients as described in the instructions.

Nigiri-Sushi with Mackerel

Spicy • Easy to prepare

Ingredients for 8 Pieces
1 fresh mackerel filet with skin about 5 oz (about 150 g) •
2 tbsp salt • $^1/_4$ cup (50 ml) rice vinegar • 1 tbsp mirin
(Japanese cooking wine) • 1 tsp sugar • 2 tsp wasabi
paste • 1 cup (150 g) prepared sushi-rice (see recipe
page 74) • 1 scallion • 1 small piece of fresh ginger
Serve with: soy sauce • wasabi paste • pickled ginger

Cooking time: 25 minutes (leave to rest for 5-6 hours)
Calories: one piece 60 calories

Wash and dry the mackerel filet. Remove any bones
with tweezers. Trim the edges. Rub the whole filet with
salt. Cover with plastic wrap and leave it to rest in the
refrigerator for 4-5 hours. Rinse off the salt under cold
running water. Dry the filet with a paper towel.

Place the filet in a flat bowl. Mix the rice vinegar, mirin
and sugar until the sugar has completely dissolved.
Pour the marinade over the filet and leave it covered
in the refrigerator for at least 30 minutes, preferably
1 hour. Turn the fish once during this time.

Remove the filet from the marinade. Pat it dry with a
paper towel. Peel the skin. Remove the skin from the
meat at the rear end. Hold the filet with one hand and
peel off the skin with the other. Cut the mackerel filet
slightly diagonally in 8 equally large pieces.

Spread some wasabi paste on one side of the filet
slices. Form the sushi-rice into 8 finger shaped rice
balls. Prepare Nigiri-Sushi as described in the
instructions.

Wash and clean the scallion. Cut into rings. Peel the
ginger and shred it. Serve the sushi decorated with
scallion and ginger.

Variation
Nigiri-Sushi with Sardines
This recipe can also be used for sardine sushi. Prepare
one 5 oz (about 150 g) fresh sardine filet with the skin
or 8 filet pieces like the mackerel filet. Rub it with salt,
let it stand for 15 minutes, rinse and marinate for 30
minutes. Unlike the mackerel, you serve sardine sushi
with the skin. Make slits in the skin with a sharp knife in
parallel lines. The contrast between the silvery shiny
skin and the fish meat is a visual delight.

Njgiri-Sushi with River Eel

More time-consuming • Exquisite

Ingredients for 8 pieces
For the eel sauce: $1/4$ cup (60 ml) soy sauce • $1/2$ cup (100 ml) mirin (Japanese cooking wine) • 1 tbsp sugar • 1 eel bone • 1 fresh river eel about $1^1/2$ lbs (about 700 g) • (Let the fish market filet the fish; remove the skin and the bones, but don't get rid of the bones.) Optional: some frying oil • 1 tbsp sesame seeds • 1 cup (150 g) sushi-rice (see recipe page 74) • 2 tsp wasabi paste • 1 toasted nori sheet • 8 long barbecue sticks
Serve with: soy sauce • wasabi paste • pickled ginger

Cooking time: $1^1/2$ hour
Calories: One piece 235 calories

Mix soy sauce, mirin and sugar for the eel-sauce in a wide saucepan. Wash and dry off the eel bone, cut into pieces and add to the ingredients. Bring to a boil and let simmer on medium to low heat for about 45 minutes until the broth turns creamy. Stir occasionally.

Meanwhile, wash and dry the eel filets. Remove any remaining bones. Cut the filets into four 5-6 inch (12-15 cm) long pieces. Put them on the sticks. In a pan, fry the eel pieces two minutes on each side in heated oil or place them side by side on aluminum foil and grill them in the oven for 5-6 minutes. Keep turning them. When ready remove the sticks and wipe off the fat with paper towel.

Put the eel sauce through a strainer. Keep 2 tbsp for later. Place the fish pieces on aluminum foil. Cover all sides with the rest of the sauce.

Toast the sesame seeds on medium heat in a pan without oil until golden brown. Cut the nori sheet into 8 strips. Form the sushi-rice into 8 logs, spread a dot of wasabi paste on them with the tip of your finger.

Make Nigiri-Sushi with the eel pieces and the rice balls as described in the instructions. Wrap a strip of the nori sheet around the middle of the sushi, stick it together with a few rice grains. Spread the rest of the spicy sauce on the eel and sprinkle it with sesame seeds.

Hints
• The eel bone adds taste to the sauce and thickens it at the same time. If you cannot use a bone, you can thicken the sauce with some cornstarch.
• If you prepare a larger quantity of eel sauce, it can be used as seasoning for squid sushi. The sauce can be kept in a sealed jar in the refrigerator for several weeks.

Nigiri-Sushi with Squid

Easy to make • In the front of picture

Ingredients for 8 Pieces
5-7 oz (150-200 g) raw, ready to use and very fresh squid tubes • 8 large whole parsley leaves • 2 tsp wasabi paste • 1 cup (150 g) prepared sushi-rice (see recipe page 74)
Serve with: soy sauce • wasabi paste • pickled ginger

Cooking time: 30 minutes
Calories: one piece 35 calories

Cut open one side of the pouch-like squid tubes. Wash and pat dry with paper towel. Spread them out flat and cut them in 8 equally large pieces about $1^1/_4$ x 2 inches (3 x 5 cm). Make three fine slits.

Wash and dry the parsley leaves. Spread a dot of wasabi paste with the tip of your finger on the smooth side of the squid, then place a parsley leaf on top. Form the sushi-rice into 8 logs. Form Nigiri-Sushi with the squid pieces and the rice as described in the instructions.

Hint
If you don't like raw squid it is possible to let it simmer in water for about three minutes. Let cool and cut into pieces.

Nigiri-Sushi with Sea Bass

In the back of picture

Ingredients for 8 pieces
5 oz (150 g) fresh sea bass filet • 2 tsp wasabi paste • 1 cup (150 g) prepared sushi-rice (see recipe page 74) • $^1/_2$-1 bunch of chives
Serve with: soy sauce • wasabi paste • pickled ginger

Cooking time: 25 minutes
Calories: one piece 40 calories

Pat the filet dry with paper towel. Remove any remaining bones with tweezers. Trim the edges with a knife. Cut the meat diagonally against the grain into 8 thin $1^1/_4$ x 2 inch slices (3 x 5 cm).

Spread a dot of wasabi paste with the top of your finger on the fish filets. Dip your hands in water and form the sushi-rice into 8 logs. Assemble the Nigiri-Sushi with the prepared ingredients as described in the instructions.

Wash and dry the chives. Decorate the sushi with two thin, long, chives each and serve immediately.

Hint
Instead of sea bass, you can use another white fish such as trout or sole.

Filled Sushi with Squid

Exquisite

Ingredients for 10-12 pieces
4 dried shiitake mushrooms • 1 medium carrot • 1 tbsp sugar • 3 tbsp soy sauce • 2 tbsp mirin (Japanese cooking wine) • $^1/_3$ oz (10 g) or a small piece of fresh ginger • 4 raw, ready to use squid tubes, about $^2/_3$ lb (300 g fresh or frozen) • 1 lime • 1 cup (125 g) prepared sushi-rice (see recipe page 74)
Serve with: soy sauce • wasabi paste • pickled ginger

Cooking time: 45 minutes (+ 20 minutes soaking time)
Calories: 12 pieces/ one piece 40 calories

Pour $^2/_3$ cup (150 ml) boiling water over the dried mushrooms and let soak for 20 minutes, then drain and retain the soaking water. Rinse the mushrooms well and discard the stems.

Wash, peel and cut the carrot lengthwise in half. Bring the soaking liquid, sugar, soy sauce and mirin to a boil in a flat saucepan. Put the mushrooms and carrot halves in the broth, cover and let simmer on medium heat for 10-12 minutes. Turn them occasionally. The carrot should be just a bit tender, not too soft.

Drain the vegetables and retain the broth. Cut the mushrooms and carrots into small cubes. Peel the ginger and cut in half.

Bring 4 cups of water (1 liter) to a boil in a pot. Add the ginger and let simmer for 4 minutes. Add the squid to the ginger water and let it boil on medium heat for about 3 minutes, until tender. Remove the squid pieces and let cool. Pat the inside and outside with paper towel and skin if necessary.

Wash the lime in hot water, pat dry with a paper towel. Cut it in half and squeeze the juice of one half. Combine the sushi-rice with the mushrooms and the carrot cubes, season with 1 tbsp vegetable broth and some lime juice. Fill the tubes with rice and cut them into 1 inch (2-3 cm) thick pieces.

Spread some broth on the fish just before serving. Take the other half of the lime, cut three thin slices and cut the slices in four small pieces. Arrange sushi and lime slices on a serving tray.

Hint
Brush the squid tubes with some eel sauce to make them tastier (see recipe page 36).

Nigiri-Sushi with Omelette

Vegetarian • For more experienced cooks

Ingredients for 8 pieces
For the omelette: 6 eggs • $1/3$ lb (75 ml) dashi (instant fish stock) • 1 tsp light soy sauce • 2 tbsp sugar • 1 pinch of salt • 1 tbsp mirin (Japanese cooking wine) • frying oil
In addition: 1 sheet toasted nori seaweed • 1 cup (150 g) prepared sushi-rice (see recipe page 74)
Serve with: soy sauce • wasabi paste • pickled ginger

Cooking time: 50 minutes
Calories: one piece 95 calories

Put the eggs for the omelette in a mixing bowl. Beat the cold dashi, soy sauce, sugar, salt and mirin until sugar and salt have completely dissolved. Add the mixture to the eggs and stir lightly, avoiding bubbles or foam.

Make an omelette from the egg mixture as described in the recipe. Fry a $3/4$ inch (2 cm) thick omelette in a greased frying pan.

Let the omelette cool down to room temperature. Then cut into two layers, so that every layer is about $1/2$ inch (1 cm) thick. Cut these in 4 even, decorative triangle-shaped pieces.

Cut the nori in eight $3/4$ inch (2 cm) thick strips. Form the sushi-rice into 8 small logs. Cover each log with a slice of omelette and press it gently together. Wrap each Nigiri-Sushi in the middle with a nori strip. Stick the ends together with some rice grains.

Hint
The omelette is easier to manage in a rectangle shaped frying pan, which you can buy in a Japanese food market. A round one works as well. It should measure about 10 inches (24-26 cm) and the sides should be high and upright. The Japanese use long chopsticks for the preparation of the omelette. If you are not comfortable with chopsticks, you can use a bendable wooden spatula.

Variation
Nigiri-Sushi with Shrimp Omelette
Add the shrimp to the egg mixture: Let 2 oz (50 g) shrimp marinate in 4 tbsp rice vinegar. Drain, pat dry with paper towel and chop into fine pieces. Add the shrimp to the egg mixture. Prepare the omelette as described in the recipe. Instead of shrimp, you can also use 2 oz (50 g) pureed fish filet.

TEMAKI-SUSHI

From Hand to Mouth

Temaki, another sushi variation, is presented in a cone form. The filling consists of cooked meat and poultry harmoniously seasoned with spicy sauces.

Every Bite a Joy

The less traditional hand-rolled Temaki-Sushi is quick and easy to prepare and tastes delicious even with less expensive fillings. Simply take a piece of nori seaweed, top it with vinegared rice and spread the filling on it. Roll the piece into a cone and serve. While professionals can do this single-handedly in one movement, it's perfectly all right to use both hands. This sushi is eaten by holding it in your hand and biting it off piece by piece. Dip the cone in soy sauce before every bite.

Fillings With No End in Sight

Temaki-Sushi may be filled with anything you feel like eating. Use any variation of fish and seafood, caviar as well as meat, poultry, vegetables, mushrooms, herbs and sprouts. Marinades for fish and meat as well as spicy sauces add even more taste to the fun.

Lettuce Instead of Nori Seaweed

If you run out of nori seaweed or as a fun variation, wrap the filling in lettuce. Use whole leaves from any green leaf lettuce such as iceberg or Boston lettuce. It is necessary, however, to tie the bottom of the lettuce cone so that the filling will not fall out. Tie the cone with thin strips of spicy pumpkin (see recipe page 12), nori seaweed, blanched carrots or leek. It's best to tie the ends of the strips after wrapping them around the cone. This is not only practical, it's also decorative. Serve the sushi shortly after completing it.

• You can purchase toasted nori seaweed or you can easily toast it yourself. Toast over medium heat in a dry frying pan until dark green and crisp.

• For a tasty snack, toast leftover nori seaweed as described above. Tear into small pieces and enjoy.

• If you'd like to fill the Temaki with semi-liquid or soft ingredients, fill the lower part of the cone with sushi-rice before topping with the ingredients.

• In Japan the fresh sprouts of daikon-radish are common ingredients for Temaki- and Maki-Sushi. If you discover the fresh sprouts in an Asian food market, bring some home. You can also get sprouts by planting the seeds of Japanese radish (giant-summer radish) in a flower pot. The sprouts have a hot, spicy taste faintly reminiscent of watercress and suits any sushi or omelette.

• You may also want to buy fresh shisho-leaves if you see them in a food market (shisho-leaves taste like a cross between mint and lemon). These are used as a garnish with white-meated fish but also do well with Temaki-Sushi with crab and avocado (see recipe page 50).

• Small Temaki-Sushi are ideal as appetizers since they are easily eaten with your fingers.

Invitation to a Sushi Party

Because Temaki-Sushi is so popular in Japan, sushi bars offer patrons a selection of ingredients so that they may assemble the Temaki themselves. This idea is perfectly suited for home entertainment. Invite your friends to a sushi party. Place everything needed on a table or a buffet. Include a large amount of nori seaweed and lettuce leaves, sushi-rice and a large tray with ingredients for a variety of fillings. You'll also need wasabi paste and pickled ginger. Don't forget bowls with vinegar water to dip your hands in. All ingredients in this book are suitable for the fillings. Each guest can assemble his or her own fillings. Half a nori sheet produces sushi the size of an ice cream cone. A quarter sheet makes sushi smaller but has the advantage of allowing you to try many different fillings.

Temaki-Sushi with Tuna and Chili-Radish

Spicy • In the front of picture

Ingredients for 4 Pieces
1 radish • 1 small dried red chili pepper • 5 oz (150 g) fresh tuna filet • 2 tbsp soy sauce • 2 tbsp mirin (Japanese cooking wine) • 1 tsp lemon juice • 2 toasted sheets of nori seaweed • 1$^1/_3$ cups (200 g) prepared sushi-rice (see recipe page 74) • 1 tsp wasabi paste
Serve with: soy sauce • wasabi paste • pickled ginger

Cooking time: 20 minutes
Calories: one piece 150 calories

Peel the radish, poke a hole in the radish and fill the hole with chili pepper. Shred radish with the chili pepper.

Pat tuna filet dry with paper towel. Cut it in $^1/_2$ inch (1 cm) strips. Mix and combine soy sauce, mirin and lemon juice. Turn the fish strips in the mixture. Squeeze out the chili-radish. Cut the nori sheets crosswise in half. Dip your hands in vinegar water and make four small balls with the sushi-rice.

Make Temaki-Sushi by placing the rice, the wasabi paste and the prepared ingredients on the nori sheet and roll it into a cone.

Temaki-Sushi with Chopped Tuna

Easy to prepare • In the back of picture

Ingredients for 4 pieces
2 fresh scallions • 5 oz (150 g) fresh tuna filet • 2 toasted nori sheets • 1$^1/_3$ cups (200 g) prepared sushi-rice (see recipe page 74) • 1 tsp wasabi paste
Serve with: soy sauce • wasabi paste • pickled ginger

Cooking time: 20 minutes
Calories: one piece 140 calories

Wash, drain and cut the scallions in pieces. Pat dry the tuna filet with a paper towel. Cut into cubes. Chop the scallion and the tuna pieces together on a plastic board with a sharp knife.

Cut the nori sheets crosswise in half. Dip your hands in vinegar water and form the sushi-rice into four small balls. Place the rice, the wasabi paste and the prepared ingredients on the nori sheet and curl it to form a cone (see instructions page 77).

Arrange and decorate the Temaki and serve at once.

Temaki-Sushi with Crab and Avocado

Child friendly • In the left of picture

Ingredients for 4 pieces.
4 small lettuce leaves • 1 small scallion • $^1/_4$ ripe avocado • 1 tsp lemon juice • 4 crab sticks • 2 toasted nori sheets • $1^1/_3$ cups (200 g) prepared sushi-rice (see recipe page 74) • 1 tsp wasabi paste
Serve with: soy sauce • wasabi paste • pickled ginger

Cooking time: 20 minutes
Calories: one piece 65 calories

Wash and dry the lettuce. Peel the scallions and cut them lengthwise in fine strips. Rinse them under water and dry with paper towel. Peel the avocado piece, cut it lengthwise in 4 strips. Brush with lemon juice.

Pat the crab sticks dry with paper towel.

Cut the nori sheets crosswise in half. Dip you hands in water and form 4 small balls with the sushi-rice.

Place the rice, the wasabi paste and the ingredients on the nori sheet and curl it to form a cone (see instructions page 77).

Temaki-Sushi with Salmon and Cucumber

Exquisite • To the right in picture

Ingredients for 4 pieces
1 piece of radish (about 50 g) • 1 piece of cucumber (about 4 inches/10 cm) • 5 oz (150 g) fresh salmon filet with skin • $^1/_2$ tbsp potato starch • 2 tbsp oil • 2 toasted nori sheets • $1^1/_3$ cups (200 g) prepared sushi-rice (see recipe page 74) • 1 tsp wasabi paste
Serve with: soy sauce • wasabi paste • pickled ginger

Cooking time; 25 minutes
Calories: one piece 175 calories

Peel the radish, slice it thinly and cut into fine strips. Wash the cucumber and cut it lengthwise into $^1/_2$ inch (1 cm) slices, then cut them, without the seeds, into short, thick strips.

Pat the salmon filet dry with a paper towel and powder it with potato starch. Fry it in a coated pan in heated oil on each side for 1-2 minutes. Place on a paper towel to absorb the fat, then cut in $^1/_2$ inch ($1^1/_2$ cm) strips. Rinse the radish in water and dry. Cut the nori sheets crosswise in half. Dip your hands in vinegar water and make 4 equally large balls with the sushi-rice.

Make Temaki-Sushi by placing the rice, the wasabi paste and the prepared ingredients on the nori sheet and form it into a cone.

Temaki-Sushi with Mixed Mushrooms

Vegetarian • Kid's favorite

Ingredients for 4 pieces
$1/_2$ lb (250 g) fresh mixed mushrooms • 4 scallions •
1 tbsp butter • 1 tbsp oil • 1 tsp soy sauce • 1 pinch of
salt • pepper • 1 tsp lemon juice • 2 toasted nori sheets
• $1^1/_3$ cups (200 g) prepared sushi-rice (see recipe
page 74) • 1 tsp wasabi paste
Serve with: soy sauce • wasabi paste • pickled ginger

Cooking time: 25 minutes
Calories: One piece 105 calories

Rub the mushrooms with a kitchen towel. Clean the caps
with a brush if needed. Wash only if necessary and let dry
on a paper towel. Slice mushrooms and remove hard
stems. Wash and clean the scallions, cut the green parts
into about 2 inch (5 cm) long pieces, then cut them into
fine strips, pat dry with paper towel.

Heat butter and oil in a big frying pan. Fry the mushrooms on medium heat until all liquid has evaporated.
Stir occasionally. Pour the soy sauce over the mushrooms and season with salt, pepper and lemon juice.

Cut the nori sheets crosswise in half using a pair of
scissors. Dip your hands in vinegar water and form
4 equally large rice balls.

Place the rice balls, the wasabi paste, scallions and
mushrooms on the nori sheet and form the Temaki-
Sushi cones.

Hint
It also looks decorative if you roll the ingredients in
lettuce leaves instead of nori seaweed. Choose perfect
green leaf lettuce like iceberg or Boston lettuce. In order
to keep the bottom of the cones together, tie them with
scallion strips or marinated pumpkin.

Temaki-Sushi with Omelette, Cucumber and Pumpkin

More time consuming • Vegetarian

Ingredients for 4 pieces
For the pumpkin: 4 dried pumpkin or dried gourd strips •
1 tsp salt • 1 tsp sugar • $1^1/_2$ tbsp soy sauce • 1 tbsp
mirin
For the omelette: 4 eggs • 4 tbsp dashi (instant fish
stock) • $^1/_2$ tsp light soy sauce • 1 tbsp sugar •
2 tsp mirin (Japanese cooking wine) • 1 pinch of salt •
oil for frying
In addition: 2 oz (50 g) cucumber • 2 toasted nori
sheets • $1^1/_3$ cups (200 g) prepared sushi-rice (see
recipe page 74)
Serve with: soy sauce • wasabi paste • pickled ginger

Cooking time: 50 minutes
Calories: one piece 180 calories

Rinse the pumpkin strips briefly under running water.
Rub them with salt until they soften. Rinse. Let soak in
warm water for at least 20 minutes.

Meanwhile, put the eggs for the omelette in a bowl. Mix
dashi, soy sauce, sugar, mirin and salt and add it to the
eggs. Stir the mixture, but don't let it get creamy or
foamy. Fry a $^3/_4$ inch (2 cm) thick omelette in a small,
preferably rectangular skillet as shown in the instructions. Remove from skillet and let cool.

Drain the pumpkin strips, cover with fresh water and
bring to a boil. Let simmer for 10 minutes. Drain.

Cover the pumpkin with fresh water. Add sugar, soy
sauce and mirin. Let simmer over medium heat, until
almost all liquid has disappeared.

Wash the cucumber and pat it dry with a paper towel.
First cut it lengthwise into $^1/_2$ inch (1 cm) strips, then cut
the strips crosswise in half. Cut the nori sheet crosswise
in half with a pair of scissors. Let the pumpkin cool and
pat dry. Cut the omelette crosswise in half, then cut into
8 equally large strips. Dip your hands in vinegar-water.
Form the sushi-rice into 4 rice balls.

Place the sushi-rice, wasabi paste, omelette, pumpkin
and cucumber strips on the nori sheets and form them
into Temaki-Sushi cones. Arrange the Temaki on a tray.

Temaki-Sushi with Chicken Breast

Spicy • Exquisite

Ingredients for 8 pieces.
For the sesame sauce: 1 tbsp dashi (instant fish stock) or water • $^1/_2$ tbsp sugar • 1 tbsp light soy sauce • 1 tsp mirin (Japanese cooking wine) • 2 tbsp sesame paste (from a jar)
In addition: 2 tbsp sesame seeds • 4 oz (100 g) chicken breast filet • one small piece of ginger about the size of a coin • 2-3 medium cabbage leaves • salt • 2 oz (50 g) whole spinach leaves • 2 toasted nori sheets • $1^1/_3$ cups (200 g) prepared sushi-rice (see recipe page 74)
Serve with: soy sauce • wasabi paste • pickled ginger

Cooking time: 45 minutes
Calories: one piece 80 calories

To make the sesame sauce, stir the dashi or water with the sugar until completely dissolved. Add soy sauce, mirin and sesame paste. Stir until smooth and creamy.

Toast the sesame seeds in a small pan without grease until golden brown. Remove from the pan.

Put the chicken breast filet in a saucepan. Almost cover with water. Peel the ginger, cut it in half and add to the chicken. Bring everything to a boil and let simmer covered on medium heat for 3 minutes.

Meanwhile, wash and clean the cabbage. Cut the leaves in small rectangles. Add the cabbage and some salt to the chicken. Let everything simmer again for 5- 7 minutes until the cabbage is tender.

Bring salt water to a boil. Wash and clean the spinach, blanch it in the boiling salt water for about 30 seconds. Rinse in ice cold water and shake it carefully.

Drain the chicken and the cabbage, rinse with ice cold water and let it drip dry. Remove the ginger. Cut the meat into small cubes, mix it well with cabbage and sesame sauce.

Cut the nori sheets into quarters. Form the sushi-rice into 8 small rice balls. Place the sushi-rice, the spinach and the chicken-cabbage mix on the nori sheet and roll it into a Temaki-Sushi cone (see instructions page 77). Sprinkle sesame seeds on the filling.

Variation
Temaki-Sushi with Pork
Prepare 4 oz (110 g) lean pork like the poultry. Instead of cabbage, cut 1 carrot in short, fine strips. Add to the meat and let it boil until "chewy". Make Temaki-Sushi as described in the recipe.

Temaki-Sushi with Beef

Very decorative

Ingredients for 4 Pieces

For the garlic-ginger sauce: 2 tbsp dashi (instant fish stock) • 3 tbsp soy sauce • 2 tbsp mirin (Japanese cooking wine) • $1/_2$ garlic clove • 1 small piece of ginger • 1 small piece of kombu (seaweed, about $1^1/_4$ x $1^1/_4$ inch/3 x 3 cm)

In addition: 1 tbsp sesame seeds • 8 small leaves of iceberg lettuce • 1 bunch of chives • $1/_2$ carrot • 1 piece of white radish • 5 oz (150 g) beef filet • salt • pepper • 2 tbsp oil • $1/_2$ toasted nori sheet • $1^1/_3$ cups (200 g) prepared sushi-rice (see recipe page 74) • 1 thin lemon slice

Serve with: soy sauce • wasabi paste • pickled ginger

Cooking time: 45 minutes (+ leave overnight)
Calories: one piece 170 calories

On the evening before serving prepare the garlic-ginger sauce. Mix the dashi with soy sauce and mirin. Peel garlic and ginger. Squeeze both with a garlic press into the sauce. Add the kombu. Let rest overnight.

The next day, remove the kombu from the sauce. Toast the sesame seeds in a small pan without any oil on medium heat until golden brown. Remove from pan.

Wash the lettuce leaves, clean, drain and pat dry with paper towel. Wash the chives and drain. Peel carrot and radish. First cut both lengthwise into thin slices, cut slices into very fine strips. Rinse the radish under cold water, pat dry with paper towel.

Dry the beef filet with a paper towel, season the whole piece with salt and pepper. Heat oil in a pan. Fry the meat on both sides on medium to maximum heat for about 2-4 minutes. Remove from pan. Remove the grease with a paper towel. Cut the beef into thin slices. Dip the slices in the garlic-ginger sauce.

Cut the nori sheets with a pair of scissors into 4 thin strips. Dip your hands in vinegar water and form the sushi-rice into 4 equally large rice balls.

Place the sushi-rice, the carrot and radish strips, beef and chives on lettuce leaves and form Temaki-Sushi.

Finally, cut the lemon slice into four pieces and stick them into the cones. Tie the bottom of the cone with a strip of nori seaweed. Spread some toasted sesame seeds on the beef.

SASHIMI&CO

Sushi Surprises

Did you know that there is sushi without rice? Or sushi that is served in a bowl with a lot of rice and delicious ingredients? Even steamed sushi is not uncommon. As you can tell, the world of sushi is full of surprises.

Sashimi

Sashimi, which means fish filet, is a type of sushi without rice. Raw fish cut in thin strips or slices melt in the mouth. In Japanese sushi bars, which are small culinary temples, sashimi is presented in beautiful arrangements decorated with artistically crafted vegetable slices. Their taste and presentation are often the highlight of a sushi meal. Sashimi is sometimes served with cooked prawns and salmon caviar. Sashimi is also suitable as an appetizer. During the meal each piece is dipped in soy sauce that is sometimes seasoned with wasabi paste.

Sashimi in Many Variations

Almost any fish is suitable for the preparation of sashimi as long as it is fresh and of the highest quality. Especially popular are sashimi made with tuna, marinated mackerel, halibut, sole, turbot, scallops and salmon. Sashimi can also be made from fresh trout. Combine the fish with spicy ingredients such as thinly sliced radish, fresh scallions and finely shredded ginger or lemon slices. The Japanese serve sushi according to the season. Fish is only used when it tastes the best. For example, coldwater fish tastes better in the fall and winter and warm water fish are more delicious during the warm months of the year.

Chirashi-Sushi

Chirashi-Sushi comes from the eastern regions of Japan and is especially popular in Tokyo. Chirashi-Sushi is the easiest sushi to make. Each diner receives a bowl filled with sushi-rice topped with a variety of raw and cooked ingredients. While the name Chirashi-Sushi literally means "spread out" sushi, this is misleading since the ingredients are carefully and artistically arranged rather than "spread out". In some Japanese provinces, however, rice and ingredients are mixed together. Since there are so many possible combinations, the preparation depends more on personal taste than on strict recipe rules. Sushi-rice for Chirashi-Sushi as well as Mushi-Sushi needs a bit more spice than the sushi-rice for other types of sushi. Simply add more rice vinegar and salt to the rice.

Enjoy the Harmony of Ingredients

Dip the rice and ingredients in soy sauce or simply drip some soy sauce on the dish. Combine ingredients and rice with every bite remembering that it's the combination that creates the taste.

Mush-Sushi – a Spicy Alternative

Most sushi is served at room temperature. Mushi-Sushi is, however, "steamed sushi" brought hot to the table. It is prepared and arranged like Chirashi-Sushi except that Mushi-Sushi is steamed briefly over boiling water. In Japan they are often served on cold days. This sushi can be reheated as leftovers in the unlikely event that there are leftovers.

Gentle Steaming

Prepare the ingredients using a two-tiered bamboo steamer approximately 9" in diameter (available in Asian food markets). The tiers can be stacked on top of each other in a pan.

Sashimi with Mixed Fish

More time consuming

Ingredients for 4 portions
For marinated mackerel: 1 whole fresh mackerel filet
with skin, about 4 oz (about 120 g) • salt • $^1/_4$ cup
(50 ml) rice vinegar • 1 tbsp mirin (Japanese cooking
wine) • 1 tsp sugar
In addition: 1 oz (30 g) kaiso kelp (dried red kelp) •
2 oz (50 g) radish • $^1/_2$ carrot • 2 oz (50 g) cucumber •
1 small lemon • a few parsley leaves • tuna and salmon
filets, 4 oz (100 g) each • 2 fresh scallops • 4 large
boiled and peeled prawns, 1 oz each (30g each) • 3 tbsp
salmon caviar • 2-4 toasted nori seaweed sheets • 4
tbsp wasabi paste

Cooking time: 1 hour (leave 4-5 hours)
Calories: one portion 160 calories

Remove any remaining fish bones with tweezers. Trim
the edges with a knife. Rub the filet with salt, cover in
plastic wrap and leave in the refrigerator for 4-5 hours.
Then rinse off the salt under running cold water. Pat the
filet dry with paper towel.

Place the mackerel filet in a flat bowl. Thoroughly stir
the rice vinegar, mirin and sugar. Pour the marinade
over the fish, cover it and place in the refrigerator for
one hour so that the fish can absorb the marinade.

Wash the dry kaiso kelp about 30 minutes before
serving. Place it in a bowl, cover with cold water
and let soak for 15 minutes.

Peel and clean the radish and the carrot. Cut both
lengthwise in thin slices and then crosswise into very
thin strips. Wash the cucumber, dry and cut it into thin
slices, then cut them in half. Cut the lemon slices in half
as well. Wash and pat dry the parsley leaves.

Remove the mackerel from the marinade and pat dry.
Skin the filet: start with separating the skin from the
flesh at the tail. Hold the fish with one hand and skin
with the other. Cut the mackerel filet diagonally across
the grain in $^1/_2$ inch (1 cm) slices.

Put the kelp in a strainer and let it drip dry. Cut tuna
and salmon filet slightly diagonally across the grain in
$^1/_2$ inch (1 cm) slices.

Arrange fish, scallops with prawns, salmon caviar, vegetables, lemon slices, nori seaweed, kaiso kelp, parsley
and wasabi paste on four wooden boards and decorate.

Chirashi-Sushi with Vegetables and Scrambled Eggs

Vegetarian • Exquisite

Ingredients for 4 portions
For the vegetables: 12 large dried shiitake mushrooms
(12-15 g) • 2 large carrots • 2 tbsp sugar • 6 tbsp soy
sauce • 4 tbsp mirin (Japanese cooking wine) • 4 slices
lotus root (from a jar) • 3 oz (80 g) pickled ginger •
salt • 1 lb (400 g) snow peas
For the eggs: 6 eggs • 2 tsp sugar • 2 tsp salt • 2 tsp
soy sauce • 8 tbsp sake (Japanese rice wine) • 1 tbsp
butter
In addition: 4-5 cups (600-800 g) warm prepared sushi-
rice (see recipe page 74)

Cooking time: 35 minutes (+20 minutes soaking time)
Calories: one portion 635 calories

Pour $1^1/_2$ cups (350 ml) boiling water over the dried
mushrooms and let soak for 20 minutes. Then pour into
a strainer. Retain the soaking water. Rinse the mushrooms well and remove the hard stems.

Peel the carrots, clean and cut once lengthwise and once
across. Bring mushroom-soaking water, sugar, soy sauce
and mirin to a boil. Let mushrooms and carrot halves
simmer in the stock for 10-12 minutes until carrots are
tender. Stir occasionally. Drain and let dry. Retain the
stock. Cut the carrots and the mushroom caps in strips.
Keep the vegetables and the stock in a warm place.

Let the lotus roots and the ginger drip dry. Bring water
and salt to a boil. Wash and clean the snow peas and let
them boil until chewy for about 3 minutes. Add the lotus
root slices for the last 30 seconds. Drain and rinse in ice
cold water. Cut the snow peas lengthwise in strips. Set
aside together with the lotus root in a warm place.

Beat the eggs together with sugar, salt, soy sauce and
sake. Heat up the butter in a coated frying pan, add the
egg mixture, bake on low heat until creamy and firm.
Stir occasionally.

Divide the sushi-rice into four tall bowls. Drip some of
the vegetable stock over it. On top of the rice arrange
scrambled eggs, snow peas, carrots and mushrooms in
a star-like fashion. For decoration place a slice of lotus
root, some pickled ginger, and some carrot and snow
pea strips in the middle.

Chirashi-Sushi with Mixed Fish

Delicious

Ingredients for 4 portions

$^1/_3$ oz (10 g) dried pumpkin or dried gourd • 1 tsp salt •
2 tsp sugar • 2-3 tbsp soy sauce • 2 tbsp mirin (Japanese
cooking wine) • 1 piece of cucumber (about 2 inches/
5 cm) • 2 oz (50 g) radish • 4 tsp wasabi paste • 4 oz
(100 g) each fresh salmon, mahi mahi and tuna filet •
4-5 cups (600-800 g) warm prepared sushi-rice (see
recipe page 74) • 4 medium or large boiled and peeled
prawns (each about 30g) • 1 tbsp salmon caviar • 3 oz
(80 g) pickled ginger

Cooking time: 40 minutes (+ 20 minutes soaking time)
Calories: 460 calories per serving

Rinse the pumpkin. Rub with salt until soft and rinse.
Let the pumpkin soak in warm water for at least 20
minutes. Drain and cover the pumpkin with fresh water,
let simmer for 10 minutes, drain.

Put the pumpkin in a saucepan and barely cover with
fresh water. Add sugar, soy sauce and mirin. Let simmer
uncovered over low heat until almost all water has
disappeared. Let cool and pat dry.

While the pumpkin is boiling, wash the cucumber, dry
and cut diagonally into wafer-thin slices. Cut them
lengthwise in half and remove the core with the seeds.
Peel the radish and cut it lengthwise into thin slices. Cut
the radish slices crosswise into wafer-thin slices. Form
the wasabi paste into four small beads, cut out a star
pattern into their upper surface.

Pat the fish filets dry with paper towels. Cut salmon and
tuna filets slightly crosswise, diagonally into $^1/_2$ inch
(1 cm) slices. Cut the mahi mahi filet the same way into
$^1/_8$ inch (2-3 mm) slices.

Divide the sushi-rice among four tall bowls. Place
salmon, tuna and mahi mahi filets on top together
with prawns, salmon caviar, pumpkin and radish strips
and arrange it decoratively with pickled ginger and
wasabi paste.

Chirashi-Sushi with Beef and Vegetables

Somewhat expensive • Spicy

Ingredients for 4 portions
For the chili-sesame sauce: 1 tbsp soy sauce • 1 tbsp sake (rice wine) • 1 tbsp mirin (Japanese cooking wine) • 1 tbsp rice vinegar • 1 tsp sesame oil • 1 tsp chili oil • 1 dash cayenne pepper • 1 tbsp sesame seeds
In addition: $2/3$-1 lb (300-400 g) marbled beef (without skin, fat or tendons) • $1^1/_2$ tbsp sesame seeds • 4 oz (100 g) each of carrot, leeks, radish and cucumber • salt • 3 tbsp oil • 4-5 cups (600-800 g) prepared sushi-rice (see recipe page 74).

Cooking time: one hour (+ let stand overnight)
Calories: 445 calories per serving

On the day before, make the chili-sesame sauce by mixing soy sauce, sake, mirin, rice vinegar, sesame oil, chili oil and cayenne pepper in a small bowl. Sprinkle with sesame seeds, cover and let stand overnight.

On the next day cut the beef into approximately $1^1/_2$ inch (4 cm) thick pieces. Wrap in aluminum foil and leave it in the freezer for 45 minutes.

Meanwhile, toast the sesame seeds in a pan without oil on medium heat until golden brown. Remove and set aside.

Wash the vegetables, clean or peel. Cut into about 2 inch (5 cm) long and $1/_4$ inch ($1/_2$ cm) thick strips. Bring salted water to a boil in a saucepan. Blanch the carrot strips in the water for 3 minutes. Add the leeks during the last minute. Drain everything and then rinse in cold water. Drip dry, cover and set aside.

Pour the chili-sesame sauce through a small strainer. Throw out the sesame seeds. Cut the lightly frozen filet slices with a large, sharp knife crosswise into equally thin $1/_8$ inch (2-3 mm) slices.

Heat the oil in a large frying pan until very hot. Brown the meat on both sides. Then add the carrot, leek, radish and cucumber strips to the beef. Add toasted sesame seeds and chili-sesame sauce. Stir everything together, season with salt and leave covered for a few minutes. Fill four deep bowls with the warm sushi-rice. Arrange the meat and vegetable mixture decoratively on top of the rice.

Steamed Sushi with Salmon and Prawns

Less complicated • More time consuming

Ingredients for 4 portions

6 dried shiitake mushrooms • $1/2$ oz (15 g) dried
pumpkin or dried gourd • salt • 1tbsp sugar • 3 tbsp
soy sauce • 2 tbsp mirin (Japanese cooking wine) •
4 oz (100 g) whole leaf spinach • 4 oz (100 g) radish
sprouts • $1/2$ lb (200 g) bamboo shoots (from a can) •
4 medium raw prawns with shell, about 1 oz each
(about 20-30 g each, fresh or frozen) • $1/2$ cup (100 ml)
rice vinegar • 1 tsp sugar • 5 oz (150 g) salmon filet
with skin • 2-3 tbsp oil • 4-5 cups (600-800 g) prepared
sushi-rice (see recipe page 74)

Cooking time: $1^1/2$ hours
Calories: 435 calories per serving

Cover the dried mushrooms with $2/3$ cup (150 ml)
boiling water. Let soak for 20 minutes. Meanwhile, rinse
the pumpkin in cold water. Rub with 1 tsp salt between
your hands until softer, rinse. Soak the pumpkin in
warm water for at least 20 minutes. Drain and cover
with fresh water. Bring to a boil and let simmer for 20
minutes. Drain. Then drain the mushrooms and retain
the soaking liquid. Rinse the mushrooms well and
remove the hard stems.

Bring mushroom-soaking water, sugar, soy sauce and
mirin to a boil. Add mushrooms and pumpkin to the
stock and let simmer covered for 15 minutes.

Remove from water and drip dry.

Bring salted water to a boil. Wash and clean the spinach
and blanch it in the boiling water for 30 seconds. Drain
and run in ice cold water, then squeeze out the water.
Wash the radish sprouts and drip dry. Cut the bamboo
shoots into $1/8$ inch (3-4 mm) thin slices.

Pin the bottom of the unfrozen or fresh prawns to a
barbecue stick to keep them from curling. Bring the rice
vinegar, $1/2$ cup (100 ml) of water and sugar to a boil. Let
the prawns boil on low heat for 3 minutes. Remove them
from the water, let them drip dry and remove the sticks.

Pat dry the salmon filet with a paper towel and cut into
four pieces. Fry them in a coated pan in heated oil on
medium heat on each side for $1/2$ a minute. Add a pinch
of salt.

Cover the bottom of a 2-tiered bamboo steamer with
aluminum foil. Pull up the sides of the aluminum foil
along the wall of the steamer. Put half of the rice in each
layer of the steamer. Spread the prepared ingredients
on top of the rice. Put the baskets on top of each other
and the lid on top of the upper basket.

Fill a wide saucepan with water (about 2 inches/5 cm).
Place the bamboo baskets inside. They should not
touch the water. It is possible to put a grid on the
bottom of the pan and place the baskets on top of it.
Bring the water to a boil and steam the sushi under a lid
on medium heat for 8-10 minutes.

Perfectly Prepared Sushi-Rice

Sushi-Rice

Ingredients for 8²/₃ cups (1300 g) prepared sushi-rice:
4 cups (600 g) sushi-rice
1 small piece of kombu (a type of kelp), about 1¹/₂ x 6 inches (about 4 x 15 cm)
¹/₃ cup (70 ml) Japanese rice vinegar
1¹/₂ tsp salt
1¹/₂ tbsp sugar

• Wash the sushi-rice under cold running water until water is completely clear, then drain.

• Fill a flat, heavy saucepan with the rice and 3 cups (700 ml) of water. Add the kombu.

• Let the rice soak for 10 minutes.

• Then bring the rice to a boil. Stir occasionally and let boil over maximum heat for 2 minutes.

• Reduce heat to the lowest flame and let the rice cook covered for 10-20 minutes, depending on package instructions.

• The rice should not overcook.

• In the meantime stir the rice vinegar with salt and sugar in a small bowl until sugar and salt have completely dissolved.

• Remove the sushi-rice from the stove. Remove the lid and cover with a kitchen towel, let cool for 10 minutes.

• Then take either a typical wooden dish (hangiri) or another shallow stoneware or unfinished wooden dish and rinse it well with cold water. Transfer the sushi-rice to the dish.

• Turn the sushi-rice quickly with a bamboo rice paddle. Sprinkle the vinegar dressing over it.

• In order to cool down quickly to room temperature and to get fluffy and shiny, draw lines in the rice with the rice paddle from left to right and from top to bottom. Don't stir and don't squeeze. Cool the rice with a fan or the rice paddle. The cooling process takes around 10 minutes. (Never put the rice in the refrigerator to cool).

• Cover the sushi-rice with a damp kitchen towel so that it does not dry out. Then use as described in the recipes.

Time and Quantity

You should calculate about 50 minutes for the preparation of sushi-rice. With this quantity you can prepare:
3 recipes of Nigiri-Sushi
1 recipe of Hosomaki-Sush
1 recipe of Futo-Maki and
1 recipe of Temaki-Sushi
Or:
1 recipe of Hosomaki-Sush
1 recipe of Gunkan-Maki a
1 recipe of Chirashi or Steamed Sushi.
Both combinations serve 4 people.

Shaping Sushi

Vinegar Water to Avoid Sticky Hands

Always have a bowl filled with vinegar water when you prepare sushi. Dip your hands in the water when you mold the rice or spread the rice on nori sheets. The vinegar water will help keep the rice from sticking. It's also helpful to cover your knife with vinegar water when you are cutting sushi rolls so that the cuts will turn out nice and smooth.

Home-Brewed Soy Sauce

A milder type of soy sauce may be served with Nigiri-Sushi or sashimi to bring out the sushi taste even more. This is how to prepare it: Dilute the dark Japanese soy sauce with water using ten parts soy sauce to one part water. Bring the combination to a quick boil. Let cool to room temperature.

Nigiri-Sushi

"Nigiri" means to "to press or squeeze". Turning rice and toppings into attractive shapes requires a gentle squeezing.

There are four different ways of forming the rice with the cylinder form being the most common in the West.

1. Fish filets are cut at a slight diagonal against the grain. Cut 8 slices which are approximately $1^1/_4$ x 2 inches (3 x 5) in size.
2. Spread a bit of wasabi paste in the middle of each fish slice. Form the sushi-rice into 8 rectangular balls.
3. If you are right handed place the first fish slice with the wasabi paste facing up in your left hand. Place a rice ball on top of the slice. With your left thumb gently press the rice down so that the rice and fish are "glued together".

4. Now take the sushi in your other hand and turn it so that the rice is facing down. Press the topping gently into the rice. Place the sushi in your

left hand again. Press the long sides gently together with your right hand to form a sushi with a rectangular shape.

5. To further perfect your sushi shape, take your right pointer finger and gently mold the sushi into a half circle.

Maki-Sushi

Using this technique you can make Hosomaki-Sushi from half a nori sheet or the thicker Futo-Maki from one nori sheet.

• For Hosomaki put half a nori sheet on a rolling mat with the smooth side of the nori down. Let the long bottom side of the nori sheet touch the bottom side of the mat.

1. Dip your hands into vinegar water. Cover the sheet with room temperature sushi-rice $\frac{1}{4}$ inch (1 cm) thick. Don't press the rice together. Leave a margin on each side of the mat. Spread a small amount of wasabi paste lengthwise on the rice.

2. Put the ingredients in the middle of the rice according to the recipe. Everything should be at room temperature except for the fish which should be cold. This will prevent the rice and the filling from sticking. Lift the bottom part of the mat and roll the nori sheet and rice around the filling to form a sushi roll. Hold the filling in the middle in order to keep it in place. Pull out the mat shortly before the roll closes.

3. Now give the sushi roll its final shape. Place a part of the rolling mat over the sushi roll, press it together gently but firmly. You can now form round or rectangular Maki-Sushi.

4. Remove the rolling mat. Put the sushi roll on the cutting board with the "seam" facing down. Squeeze the open ends together with your fingers. Dip a large, sharp knife in vinegar water. Cut the sushi roll in half.

5. Put the two halves next to each other and cut them equally in half or in three parts, according to the recipe. You can cut either straight or diagonally. You will have 4 larger or 6 smaller pieces. Place the Maki-Sushi upright and decorate.

Gunkan-Maki

Only fillings of soft consistency (for example, salmon caviar) are used in Gunkan-Maki. The fillings are held together by a "wall" of nori seaweed.

1. Dip your hands in the vinegar water and make 8 finger shaped rice balls from the sushi-rice. Wrap a strip of nori seaweed around each rice ball with the smooth side facing out. Glue the strip together with several rice grains.

2. Carefully press the rice down inside the circle of seaweed. Top it with the filling according to the recipe and decorate the Gunkan-Maki.

Ura-Maki-Sushi

"Inside-out" sushi requires a little more attention when assembled. The extra work, however, is rewarded with especially decorative sushi (for example, California roll).

• Wrap plastic foil around a rolling mat so that the rice will not stick to the mat. Wet the foil with some vinegar water.

• If you don't have a mat, use strong aluminum foil sprinkled with vinegar water in place of the mat and the plastic foil. Place half a nori sheet with the smooth side down on the mat. Make certain that the bottom edge

of the sheet meets the edge of the mat.

• Dip your hands in vinegar water. Cover the nori sheet with $1/4$ inch (1 cm) thick layer of warm sushi-rice. Don't squeeze the rice. Leave a margin on all sides.
1. Flip the nori sheet around so that the rice is now facing the mat. Spread some mayonnaise along the middle of the nori. Then place the filling on top.
2. Roll the sheet with the mat and press it together like Maki-Sushi. Take a sharp knife, dip it in vinegar water and cut the roll in half. Place the halves next to each other and cut into three pieces so that you now have 6 sushi pieces. Dip one side of each sushi piece in toasted sesame seeds. Place upright and decorate.

Temaki-Sushi

Temaki-Sushi is made into cones from either $1/2$ or $1/4$ of a nori sheet depending on desired size.

• Dip your hands in vinegar water and make 4 or 8 balls from the sushi-rice depending on the recipe. Place the nori sheet in your left hand with the smooth side facing down.

1. Place a rice ball on the upper end of the nori. Spread some wasabi paste on the rice. Place $1/4$ or $1/8$ of the filling on the rice (for example, salmon, cucumber and radish) and press gently so that the filling and rice stick together.

2. Roll the nori sheet with the filling into a cone with a pinched bottom so that the filling will not slip out. Place a few rice grains on the outside of the cone to act as a "glue" to hold the cone together.

Helpful Hints in the Sushi-Kitchen

How to Make the Omelette Work

The Japanese use a special rectangular frying pan for the preparation of the omelette. It is also possible to use a round coated 10 inch (24-26 cm) pan.

• First, heat 3 tbsp oil in a pan over strong heat. Tilt the pan back and forth so that the oil covers the base evenly. Then remove the oil from the pan.

• Pour a thin layer of the egg mixture and let it set over medium heat. Get rid of any bubbles that occur. Use a wooden spatula and fold the omelette once. It should now be about $2^1/_2$ inches (6 cm) wide.
1. Brush the free space in the pan with some oil. Again cover it with some of the egg mixture. Lift up the first part of the omelette and allow it to absorb some of the liquid.
2. Let the second part set, but leave a shiny surface.
3. Then roll the first piece of the omelette around the new one until all egg mixture has been absorbed.

• Lift the finished omelette which should be about $3/_4$

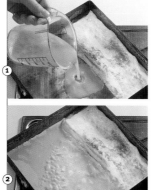

inch (2 cm) thick from the pan and place it on a cutting board. Let cool. Then cut it according to recipe into decorative pieces.

What to Eat Before and During the Sushi Meal

Sweet-Sour Vegetable Strips
Ingredients for 4 portions:
$3^1/_2$ oz (100g) each of white radish, carrot and cucumber, 1 tbsp salt, 1 piece of lemon peel (organic), $^1/_4$ cup (60 ml) rice vinegar, $^1/_4$ cup (50 g) sugar, 1 tsp fresh shredded ginger.

Wash the vegetables, peel and cut into very fine sticks about $1^1/_2$ inches (4 cm) long. Mix with salt, set aside for 10 minutes. Then rinse well and pat dry. Cut the lemon peel into wafer-thin strips. Bring vinegar, sugar, lemon peel and ginger to a boil. Pour over vegetables. Marinate 1 hour. Stir occasionally. You can keep the vegetables covered in the refrigerator up to 5 days.

Spinach Salad with Sesame Sauce
Ingredients for 4 portions: 1 lb (400g) whole leaf spinach, salt, 2 tsp peeled sesame seeds, 2 tbsp sesame paste (from a jar), 2 tbsp light soy sauce, 2 tbsp dashi (instant fish stock) or water, $^1/_2$ tsp sugar.

Wash the spinach and blanch for 1 minute in boiling salt water, drain, run in cold water and let drip dry. Toas the sesame seeds in a pan without oil. Stir sesame pa; with soy sauce, dashi or water. Turn the spinach in t sauce, season with salt and sprinkle with sesame seeds

Miso Soup with Tofu
For 4 portions:
$3^1/_3$ cups (800 ml) dashi (instant fish stock), 2 scallions, 7 oz (200 g) firm tofu, $3^1/_2$ oz (100 g) miso (soybean paste), 1 tbsp sak (Japanese rice wine), salt.

Bring dashi to a boil. Wash the scallions and cut in wafer-thin slices. Cut the to into cubes. Stir in miso wit some dashi. Add it togethe with sake to the rest of the broth, stir until smooth. He up tofu and scallions in the broth for 5 minutes, seasor with salt.

Index